THE
PASSION
& THE
POETRY

THE
PASSION
& THE
POETRY

Christine Store
Stratford 2013
God Friday

by

Geneva M. Neale (Audain)

iUniverse, Inc.
Bloomington

The Passion & The Poetry

iUniverse books may be ordered through booksellers or by contacting:

iUniverse
1663 Liberty Drive
Bloomington, IN 47403
www.iuniverse.com
1-800-Authors (1-800-288-4677)

ISBN: 978-1-4759-2535-7 (sc)
ISBN: 978-1-4759-2536-4 (ebk)

Printed in the United States of America

iUniverse rev. date: 11/19/2012

CONTENTS

ACKNOWLEDGMENTS

Video Producer, Photographer, Film maker Graham Gordon, 2007
Website Developer Coordinator Robert Niven, 2007, 2012
without these professionals I would not have achieved any
organization of this book goal setting.

As Past President of Access Toastmasters International Club.
I acknowledge these Presidents who preceded me who watch
my growth

Thaddeus Stewart, Joy Stewart, Mary Helwig-Hall, Beatrice
Mclean, President of ACCESS, Charter members of ACCESS
Club. sponsored by Afro Canadian Caribbean Association
organization.
McMaster Toastmaster—Jonathan Speigel, Past President,
District 86 PR 2010
Dundas Ontario, Canada, Valley Town Toastmasters Club, Tony
Bradshaw, Past President and Executive member of Toastmaster
District 86 and each member of this club.
Nelson Blanco Ruiz, District Governor 2009-2010 Exectutive
Toastmasters International District 86.
Leadership communication certification.
Toastmaster International Clubs Competitions: Speeches and
Evaluations Contests, Humorous Contests, Table Topics Contest
major tasks. Districts Schools.
I appreciate each members' evaluations over 60 Speeches from
Advance Manuals.
Communication polished my ability to speak with confidence
by using Props, illustrative Charts or Power Points.
Being designated to a term as Area 53 Governor for District 86
boosted decision making skills.
I fulfilled and exceeded Leadership management roles for four
Toastmasters clubs.

Enhancements which contributed as my relaxed mode of thinking, envisioning and rolling out my entrepreneur mode by publishing THE PASSION & THE POETRY Volume One in 2012

Copyright edition of Geneva M. Neale (Audain)

Passionate soul my grand children Maxwell and Gabrielle Majewski. Siona Neale Majewski, Colette Neale.

Smiles to friends and families and every one of my good, good friends Trinidad and Tobago and adopted resident, Merle Nelson of Canada.

HAYDAIN NEALE

Haydain you always called to tell me.
Where jacksoul band gigs happening location.
As far as Montreal to Vancouver in Canada.
Even got your card from Japan July 27, 2007.
August 3, 2009 accident stopped me cold.
Communication continued in Sacred Silence.
jacksoul band members believed in sojourner.
Mission Statements posted at your bedside.
Cause and effect recoup principles foremost.
My son jacksoul inseminate world visions.
You motivated momsy in jacksoul sessions
    specials.
Spoke with passions momsy's ethics black
    history.
Principals of mother's choice of musical
    influences.
Napoleon Hill and Universal Unity acceptance
    of all.
My son for your everlasting love Peace unfolds.
Many names for God you never query ACTS.
Yaz and Michaela Hudson Neale marital family.
Bye bye bye "Little Bird You Are Welcome"
    lullaby.
You remembered I will continue to hum
    peacefully.

HAYDAIN NEALE
jacksoul R&B band Lead Singer

Forever in MOMSY body, mind and soul thoughts.
My only man child is at rest November 22, 2009.

Copyright Geneva M. Neale (Audain)

MY FIRST EASTER 2010

Nah man, No Chocolate rabbits. Easter 2010
Easter Home thulium yes, man ah just made some man.
What chocolate rabbit? No, ah ha, chocolate tea too booth.
Market time, buy a real instant rabbit, make a curry stew.
It dawned on me for the first time today "ah doh have no son."
Wait a minute Haydain is not with us to invite me to his home.
Haydain has gone over yonder playing Savannah concerts.
No box of turtles from him this Easter for
   "meh to chew."
Nor visiting his home for aperitifs of "various types of cheese."
Turtles are my favorite everyday chocolates nuts to chew.
I then went to the freezer took out some blended coconut.
Got the Molasses out added it to the coconut and sugar.
Made my own Trinidad and Tobago molasses thulium.
   "Foh soh."
I wondered as I stirred the candy bubbling up Volcanic glob,"
   ah well! My son is gone".
Haydain is over yonder in his heaven and so he like Christ is risen.

Here I am in this Hamilton heaven enjoying life making
   sweeties
My daughter who lives with me could not wait for coconut
   treats.
As soon as I completed this new found hobby.
   Home made candies.
Before yoh say "chocolate jack rabbit" been snacking on molasses
   thulium's.
There is light at the end of this heavenly tunnel.
   Haydain's illuminations.
These molasses macaroon that is what it is called in Canada.
Molasses is sweet in the mouth soon will come out at the end.

Copyright Geneva M. Neale (Audain) My first Easter 2010

Successful Musician Songwriter Memorialized by his sister

Haydain Neale was born in Hamilton, Ontario, the youngest of 4 children. Neale is survived by his 3 sisters.

Music was fundamental to the ancestry of the Neale–Audain family. It was only natural that Haydain Neale became interested in music at an early age, beginning with the piano and the violin. From this exposure, he was soon composing and performing, forming a band with childhood friends. This progressed into something which could be shared with the world: jacksoul.

Jacksoul, was a Toronto based, R&B band with Neale as the lead singer. Haydain Neale made his first public appearance at Bravo's Mowtown At The Concert Hall. Neale penned many award-winning, Canadian R&B hits (e.g. hits Can't Stop and Still Believe in Love)

However, Neale's talent was also recognized in his ability to interpret classic soul songs. Jacksoul's acclaimed album "Resurrected" put a new on twist on works by Radiohead, Curtis Mayfield and Sam Cooke, setting a standard by which all new R&B artists would have to measure themselves.

He went on to win 3 Juno Awards, one of which was awarded posthumously following his premature death at age 39.

In August 2007, Haydain Neale sustained serious injuries in a motorcycle accident. After a long recovery from that crash, which saw him return to the studio to complete what would be his final album (under circumstances which bore witness to his incredible inner strength and musicality)

Haydain Neale was diagnosed with a rare form of throat cancer—despite the fact that he had never smoked in his life.

Haydain Neale, whose personal life had always been characterized by the highest rectitude of conduct and wonderful humility—garnering him respect worldwide—succumbed to complications resulting in November 2009. This insert pays tribute to Neale's brilliance, enduring inspiration and the memory of his mother.

I do expect questions as to why I wrote a few of my poems in island dialect or twang.

I was born and grew up in The Republic of Trinidad & Tobago.

DIALECT IS FIGURATIVELY CORRECT

"GRAMATICAL SPINS ON the formal English studied at High school"

Sweet RHYTHYMIC METAPHORES echoes off islanders abroad and at home.

If I do not observe tradition then I am truly lost.

Then it is a burning shame that I was born a "Trine".

I am a graduate from secondary school, university and college.

I live in Canada since 1965. I am a Citizen of Canada.

"AH DOES TALK GOOD, GOOD, GOOD." Rhythm, tone and sound.

Copyright Geneva M. Neale (Audain) May 24, 2012

ECOLOGY

I never knew that the water that surrounds Trinidad and Tobago would be classified as an ecology studies faculty.

As a child I feared the Atlantic Ocean which surrounds the Islands. I lived with my grandparents who live a stone throw away from the oceanfront. The colours of the sky, the clouds that surrounded the moon and tides in and outs surfs in the ocean translated as time, as the weather man or the barometer obtained in the brute strengths of the forces of the blowing winds. Hence my poem about the psychology of the psychological effect on me as a child.

It is about the changes of the either friendliness or the angered bellowing of the ocean tearing away at the natural shorelines. The fears of the ocean taking my grandfather away and not bringing him back from his fishing expeditions because the banks were being torn apart because of the constant bashing of the surfs against the sea walls.

In this century, it is the real estate that surrounds the high priced business of selling ocean front properties that is having a psychological effect of global warming not only caused by man but by the natural causes and effects of nature.

Geneva M. Neale (Audain)

DRATS

Cold draft slap like waves against faces.
Grey clouds drape like chiffon floating sky.
Thunderous blasts shuddering cosmic hideouts.
Infatuation beams touch body, mind or soul.
Weather forecasters wave magic digital wands.
Shake their heads as picture today is bland.

Uninspired forecasts as barometers plummet?
Viewers as amused George Burns poems claimed.
What is happening to forecasts worldwide?
Weather cocks revolve atop garages theatre.
Cocks swing north, east, west or south.
Steam pours identically as chute on trains.

Sidewalks transformed ice rink compactness.
Salt cannot melt falling snow flakes.
Yearly is said the worst barometric study.
Global warming makes no sense body freezes.

Temperatures fluctuate or escalate cyclic.
Icicles dazzling diamonds sub-zero storms.
Seasonal clothing wear seasonal displays.
Wardrobes designed fashion performances.
Layered seasonal trends slap drafts of air.

Copyright © 2009 Geneva M. Neale (Audain)

ECO-PSYCHOLOGY

Books on oceanic geography studied.
Shore lines sounds barriers boomed.

Constructoral machines erections clanged.
Demolitions legislations people enraged.

Coves curves, inlets, rivulets slushing.
Mountainous barriers groans distorted.

Bulldozing rocky cliffs while ocean filled.
Artificial sand-filled shorelines shamed.

Eco friendly teams of ecologists streamed.
Renound ecology psychologists swarmed.

Questions need answers symbologists sustained.
Emphatic sounds of rocks erosions stumped.

Craftily conceal high staked investors dreamed.
Landfills scientists researchers samples unseen.

Forced relaxed mood swings controls intacted.
Can earth smile when all guidelines are pinged?

Eco-psychology lab analysis shores be protected.

ICICLE

Memories of assortments on ice canvas.
Ice storm maze patterns an amazement.

Frozen sculpted shapes world renown.
Braided ice-covered panes glisten.

Nature's patio transformed glaciers.
White sandy textured hale pop sounds.

Fascination as rain on snow blend.
Thoughts waltz as nature pantomimed

Sculptures blink as blue sapphires.
Screen-prints icy grains quietly spin.

Snow piled as patio table cackled.
Translucent figurine two-feet tall.

Mystic hands shaped skating rink.
Snowman imaginative chisels cling.

Beautiful scenic view paints ambiance.
Carvings resemble orchestra.

Picture Rhinestone instruments.
Classical illusion music ride waves.

Iced cellos, timbers, flutes whisper.
Harmonious base reverberations scream.

Copyright © 2009 Geneva M. Neale (Audain)

ODE TO MOTHERS

Both grandparents owned ground provisions properties.
Grand ma Berta danced tons of cocoa and coffee beans.
Grand ma Lilly managed long term liabilities.
Grandpa Scott wallowed profits cured tabbaco leafs.
Berta birth to five siblings who excelled in school.
Lilly bless her soul and ten great skilled traders.

Both dads waited patiently for V Day celebrations.
Overheads were not prevalent in those days Zeppelins
Stocks and bonds markets cash flows or goats and pigs.
No commissions of income taxes in the fifties.
Children counted their marbles proprietorship's.
Mothers operatives teams fair winners or soar lossers.

Revenue holders, referees if children got swindled.
Moms calculated cost of marbles and ring designs.
Dads stooped to mentor neighbourhood disruptive kids.
Ambassadors cooled tempers with fresh baked breads.
Moms solved problems before children got into fights.
Red carnations for deceased, white for moms alive.

Teachers annually coached class to SOLEMNLY recite.
MOTHERS' ODE the poem I sing loudly on Mother's Day.

SOLAR

Life a field of ripened surprises.
Warm water swirls around panels.
Solar panels on top house roofs.
Package reduced at a home show.

Both solar panels now installed.
Kitchen transforms to sunny indoors.
Morning, noon and night brilliance.
Investment cost shines through.

Imagine outdoors turned inside out.
Excited no longer dine in darkness.
God's natural elements flavoured.
Solar panels modern era venture.

EMANCIPATION

Geneva found that the principles as used by Napoleon Hill philosophies in the book "Think And Grow Rich" made a lot of sense. He used bible principles.

Think and Grow Rich: A Black Choice, by Dennis Kimbro's book (co-authored with Napoleon Hill) reveals the secrets to success of many of America's most successful African-Americans.

ADOLESCENCE

Young adults, sons-in-law

Young adults excel balance networks.
Young adults powered individuals.
Multi-races sons-in-law family trees.
Sons or daughters family dynasty.

Active structural decisions beams.
Successful behaviors cultivate.
Journal creative assessments goals.
Activate minuscule cells goals.

Relax great leader Nelson Mandela.
Seniority flaunt ownership maturity.
Evacuate international confidential.
Debate flamboyant armies adolescence.

Colour Astrophysical

Bobby de Silighi art astrophysical colours.
Captured planetary star shooting experiences.
Bobby's cosmic life ended January 14, 2009.
Today I knelt at wisdom's space in silence.
Mourners' memories of oil paint pallets fragrance.
Nature noteworthy cosmic woman left us.
Commentaries extra terrestrially primed.
She wrote poetry that captures astragal beauty.
Cosmic poetry book of light-years drapes and veils
Paintings hues of cosmic dramas drew deep sighs.
Another demonstration of her Art work recital.

As if waiting students in famous Art Galleries.
Every one who came to bid Bobby's strengths adieu.
A wonderful woman life-time was lying now in state.
Wonderful tall tales in relation to Bobby a character.
"Cosmic castrations" a phrase to all men she bellowed.
Bobby's attention getter men never got its translation.
A wreath of scarlet roses adorned her casket an eye catcher.
Bobby seemed as though she sat on her cosmic throne.
On a panel perhaps or an Art Studies cosmic lecture
Waterdown, Ontario Bobby judged Art talent searches.
Astral Artist lectured in Johannesburg, South Africa.
Mandela was incarcerated breaking quarry stones.

CULTURE MIX

Life is beautiful foever.
Observe talented marketers.
Circumvent millions of demands.
Flat bed big wheels deals.

Farmers mode of transportation mules.
Through ice storms blurriness.
From which gratefully return.
Workers emerge rarely frost bitten.

So much for sharing gloves.
With myths that energize.
Bright flare for agriculture.
Concur with news about Mount Everest.

Mystics metaphysics heal cold sores.
For whom I will give my awl.
Teachings that moderate attitudes.
Billions bleating souls mourn.

Sow seeds of positives outreach.
Rural lifestyles layered leer.
Truths attributes displays.
Universality cultures mix.

MIRROR

Light stare in the mirror impulsively.
That feature does look like mine inquiringly.
My reflection looks naked memories regenerated.
My childhood days cascades.
Cascade villagers stretch out on river stones.
Youths gathered to bathe as arguments exceed ripples.
Rocks, pebbles, stones sediments.

Nakedness invisibility.
No alarms go off nor do Tata tales sound bite.
Neighbours children expectations stories silenced.
Soaking wet clothes get stone washed.
Normal process of families daily tasks.
Fashionable meeting places down by the river.
Riversides gathering of almost naked individuals.

Puberty wash ashore laze around river banks.
Villages mothers and fathers voices celebrated.
Neighbours status quo well-known.
Not one child dare cross expectations boundaries.
Foreigners cannot understand natives nakedness.
As watchful eyes stare inquisitively

R. R. RHODES

Set director watches the set construction.
The Actors wait! Leads stage Right entrance.
The stage crew on cue lights out, headset on.
Butterflies in stomachs lights switched low.

Turn your back on your audience suspension.
Production director shouts listen to me.
Pitch your voice like a baseball bat swings.
The cast picks up all moods swings! Action.

Rhythm, keep dramatic effects in character.
Defence, quality, face each other, walk away.
On stage use your opportunity to pause.
Don't give the audience your backs. Plotting.

Look out through your audience! Not at them.
Head thrown back, head lowered half turned,
Quizzical questioning looks, reaction BAM.
The audience just went wild, encore, encore.

Stage crew pay attention! No inconsistancy.
Actors observe the opportunities to pause.
Do not lose your concentration dancers.
Encore, Dinner Theatre bar last call, close.

Rainy Day Innocence

Poised to read another of my poems.

My smile fits tender tropical fruits.
I hardly hear rain drops in Canada.
Asphalt insulation soften drops.

Rain drops noises squirreled away.
Beeps of high blood pressure pulse.
Or raining criticism of feed backs.
I wish I can tell my naked rainy tale.

Children skins with water bubbles.
My ancient memory laughs as I recall.
Children laugh excitedly in the rain.
Titled Innocent Rainy Shower Baths.

Picture as I read my passionate poems.
Must add 'bout Grand ma's witty laughs.
Grandma's Marble Games chip as showers of rain.

Copyright © 2009 Geneva M Neale (Audain)

Spin off Emancipation 200 years

African birthright spin-offs diligence attributes.
Ebony bows on board middle passage slavery trades.
Tribal arrows adorn transcontinental ships.

Nothing frazzled watchful slaves predestinations.
Strategic patterns fused shipments authentication.
Wisdom mastered trachea tubbiness groans.

Envoys designed passageway compartments.
Medical teams astonished gasps man overboard.
Captain's logged anarchy projections concerns.

Slave traders turf out societal barricades.
Sugarcanes field a smoothed burning mess.
Penetrate creepy-crawly slave internments.

His warmth within her kinfolk's URN burnt.
A vintage hot rod he skilfully reclaimed.
The paint job he completes proudly on time.

Mom shrouds his soul's pottery in her arms.
His African ancestors celestial body renewed.
Final breaths syncopated transcendental waves.

He smiles. Hamilton's Harbour sandy waves bellow.
Mom beholds Africa's brave young man spirit rays.

UNTITLED

His body layed out gracefully status ebony.

Sketches confligurations circulated HIS mind.

Juju warrior selected feathers jourvert morn.

African civilization dynasties ablaze ablaze.

History jump up in Trinidad sweet sweet pan.

Trinidad's sister island Tobago so esoteric.

Uncle Polly with majestic peacocks plumes.

Last lap means "bambai until we meet again."

Ash Wednesday escalate up St. Peter's Gate.

ATheist, calypso massman, HONOUR HIS URN.

Breadfruit Sans Coche Trinidad&Tobago melee.

Good Heaven Polly's 7 feet tall soul arrives.

Copyright © 2007 Geneva M. Neale (Audain)

EMOTIONS

Many of Geneva's poems are based on emotions, the ups and downs of everyday life which we all feel . . . . That is what makes us ALIVE!

Global Issues

Today I write poetry about "Global Unison Issues" as published in the International Society of Poetry Anthology.

- From each decade as we acquire knowledge we gleam from quotes "Sages from each tribes who told their unique creation stories through prayer wheels, beads, temples, mountain top structures and fictions histories of the books' world."

- I used to think that my grandparents used to be sitting in Africa or India or China or Sera since these were the people who lived in neigh villages.

- One Friday night per month the elders swapped legends about the sea voyages as fishermen or co-operative committees.

- They were either pleased with or ticked off with the Foreign Aid Medical Health Teams that served each County which made these intelligent villagers give their advice.

- T Stories told and retold about the after effects of the slave traders or the benefits gained after slavery, emancipation of slave William Wilberforce, William Pitt and the guy who wrote Amazing Grace.

- The Indentured labourers from India and China and Sera merchants or merchants peddling provisions from every Island.

- Foreign Freight that came into Trinidad for transportation of Trinidad and Tobago crude oil shipments or the asphalt abundance off our Pitch Lake.

- St. Vincent, Montserrat, Grenada, Barbados, Dominica, St. Lucia, St Kitts these are Islands of either the Windward as well as the Leeward Caribbean Islands. We closely related to British Guyana down the mainland of Venezuela in South America ancestors boarded boats to bring goods to Trinidad.

Stories about windjammers or tall ships, schooners or fishing boats they spoke about maintaining good County job which they did as employers or employees

70TH BIRTHDAY 2010

I thank every one for my 70th birthday wishes,
Each thoughtfulness and memories;
We have shared over the 25 or more years.

My 70th year 2010 story teller presence.
Celebratory years tall as matured bull rushes.
Cultivate natures natural forces techniques.

45 years a Canadian citizen arrived in 1965.

Ducks waddle in poetic streams sing happy songs.
Bulrushes adorn banks hide pikes or even salmon.

Slipping over gray pebbles that resemble cat fish.
Throughout stony white waterways schooners rise.
Tumbling waters—stop abruptly before invasive rocks.

Shapes off native stone sculptured figures mid stream.
While disturbed sediments settle like crocodiles.
Water rise up or down engineered Erie Canal locks.

As sands of time capture water logged trapped logs.
Poetry is used in Humanities armorous logged tales.
A son who rise to JUNO fame struck near a traffic light.

Swept away by tides off subtle neon waves.
Good bye my son memories savory tastes live on.
Iconic visionary portraits adorn momsy's mind.

Copyright Geneva M. Neale (Audain)

CEASEFIRES

Understandings, wisdom, TRUTHS.
Love indoctrinated national pride.
Blessings to all who make soldiers.
Truths soldiers choice pray ceasefires.

Today understand the wisdom philosophies.
In Truths mental breakdowns psychologies.
Values in silence, service in wisdom.
God prayers in envelopes sent not received.

Miles and miles of bible verses teach.
Students study David's triumphs and deaths.
Abraham Lincoln parliamentary process.
His inaugural Slavery Freedom speech.

Wilberforce, Newton, Wesley, Cabot debated.
Holy wars triumphs in songs hundreds recorded.
Oh my God soldiers fight Freedom's fights.
Soldiers enlist accomplish Global Peace.

GLOBAL UNISON

One voice of inspiration.
One final compressed tone.
Thousands' last breaths uttered.
Acclimatized insightfulness.

Twin Towers' cenotaph eulogize.
"Accouchez" stunned actuaries.
Bodies, minds, souls depart.
Optimize emergence endurance.

United States America compassions.
Will families forgive this pain?
New era 9/11 2001 rebuilds.
Universal affability sustain?

Honey Moon

Prepare for pro-creation.
Human science systems air bound.
Blast off like rockets in space.
Fuel burn off another eclipse.
Parents beaming psalms solutions.

Mother, Father giver wedding daze.
Wedding ceremonies brides in white.
Sights affixed salty tears impaired.
Another son or daughter honey moon.
Life after birth fore mentioned.

Layette blue, pink or neutral instead.
Take home child bundled up in blanket.
Kindergarten express learn, learn.
College, university independent system.
Myths, philosophers' mind expansions.

MAPLE

Who would have thought
simple trees destined to be
Symbols of Unity
all countries

Maple trees in Canada
Chaconia in La Trinity
An island in the Caribbean

Dignity, loyalty, beauty
cultres of diversities

World wide web as trees
Circumvent all countries
spiders spins the net or web
Hats off! Pride hidden in
all national trees
Flags? Universal national trees

Copyright © 2007 GENEVA M. NEALE

REMEMBER ME DAY

RE-MEMBER ME 11 11 2002, Every day of each year.

I saw some veterans yesterday speaking about 2nd World War.
Many had tears flowing down their cheeks.
I thought of Silent Unity.
Each veterans said to me "Pray Silently for me"

Today we hear cries of wars, wars, wars.
The possible invasion somewhere in the middle east.
40 years from now would we regret again?
Yet again and again?

Thank you God for the illumination.
The elimination of all wars especially World War 3.
Thank You God. Prayers work, Silent Unity.
You see I was born 11 05 1940.

TRENDS

"How Black Are We?" A heat wave.
Listen to Smokey Robinson's Address.
As he smokes out Race Naming Errors.
Families spaced out racially divided.
Terminologies for mixtures of genes.
Color wheels ticking back and forth.
Stop insults of grandma's ancestors.

I do feel white washed or discolored.
"Grandma I do not like you." Why?
I look away my face various colors.
Why! "You are not as white as my mom."
Your skin does not look as my dad's.
Why are you so Black?

Incredible phenomenon grandchildren.
Easter is about African Easter lilies which also comes in red.
Smokey takes on America's trends.
NAACP race all Americans debates.
African American colored people.
African Caribbean Canadian long lists.

Trinidad & Tobago's African Canadian?
Since I live in Canada I AM a CANADIAN.

METAPHYSICS

Metaphysics, a branch of philosophy that explores truths and sharpens knowledge, also caught Geneva's interest.

For 31 years, Geneva studied the various metaphysical principles. These were five easy steps which made her shout "hurrah I have got ideas just like Emmet Fox, Aristotle. Einstein."

Geneva often goes through the philosophers writings who have helped to brighten her days. As each philosophy fans and touches a specific idea in her head, it grows into poetry.

Enlightenment took Geneva back to school at age 34 in 1974. Grade 13, College, Night School, finally got her University juices flowing and she graduated after 10 years of Continuing Education at McMaster University in Human Services Management.

These philosophies empowered her to lose her fears. "The carrot and the stick" lessons by Abraham Maslow became her mantra for her to conquer each fear. Geneva paid attention to build skill while she began transforming her cultural thinking ways to positive enhancements tools.

Abraham Maslow
"This is a refreshing change from the theory X of Freud, by a fellow psychologist, Abraham Maslow. Maslow totally rejects the dark and dingy Freudian basement and takes us out into the fresh, open, sunny and cheerful atmosphere. He is the main founder of the humanistic school or the third force which holds that all the good qualities are inherent in people, at least, at birth, although later they are gradually lost."

ARAMAIC LANGUAGE

First spring—cleaning remove the stone.
Christ resurrected from the borrowed tomb.
Aramaic language words were misunderstood?
Squandered energies hates, fears or angers.
What is the greatest directive but Love.
Christ dishonored was crucified and died.
Spring—clean each mind with confidence.
Meditate prune negative weakened hearts.
Highlight positives beautify spiritual souls.
International observations each Easter morn.
Christ's Aramaic words 'The Be Attitudes.'
Wisdom "In the beginning the word." Aramaic.

CHOCOLATE EAGLE WINGS

Chocolate Eagle perched on satellite dish.
Cultural interpretations as subtitles breeze flutter.
Chocolate colored eagle joyfully alights.

Omens visionary successful brain injuries recovery.
August 2007 fete Caribana distilled with anxieties.
Mega watts cerebral surgeries treatments. an ordeal.

World wide web hits as universe fans embraced.
Painful therapeutics expedition tubes placements.
Body organs ducts for fluid intakes sealed outputs.

Envision world wide supplications abound revitalize.
As stars maneuver jacksoul lives within emails vigils.
Four months asleep a chocolate eagle's dreaminess.

Magnetic rays expressions from mom to Haydain . . .
Masterminders relativity during advent holy days.
Thy will be done son as four continents winds blow.

Thy will in every faiths Father deliver earthly son.
Extended families unified oneness in love expressions.
Hands reach as grapes vines in vineyards weave.

Nations hugged and kissed and hugged our open arms.
Fanfares of tearful buckets pulled from inner wells.
Weeks of healing tears mom feelings are dehydrated.

The chocolate eagle my son survived a fractured skull.
Traumatic experience as the chocolate eagles alight.
Jacksoul's spiritually singing renewals perchance hums

CULTURES MIX

Life is beautiful foever.
Observe talented marketers.
Circumvent millions of demands.
Flat bed big wheels deals.

Farmers mode of transportation mules.
Through ice storms blurriness.
From which gratefully return.
Workers emerge rarely frost bitten.

So much for sharing gloves.
With myths that energize.
Bright flare for agriculture.
Concur with news about Mount Everest.

Mystics metaphysics heal cold sores.
For whom I will give my awl.
Teachings that moderate attitudes.
Billions bleating souls mourn.

Sow seeds of positives outreach.
Rural lifestyles layered leer.
Truths attributes displays.
Universality cultures mix.

Digital lights

Xmas is about forgiveness candle lights.
Exiting doubts or fears replaced happiness.
Globally stars shine bright all see eye to eye.
Lights of God stars illuminate us all.
Electrical lights shine beyond and above.

Enlighten our darkness universal God.
Christ meant Christ followers globally.
Religions sow diverse patterns of Peace.
BATTLERS call ceasefire on Holy days.
One GOD prayers Oneness Peace always.

Disagreement with pilgrim's covenants.
Oriental lanterns twinkling golden glows.
Celebrations in religious set teachings.
Festival of Lights throughout the universe.
India's scented oils incensed spirits light.

Digital candles float down rivers of the worlds.
Festivals of essence at Buddhists ceremonies.
India's Ganges, African River Niles geography.
Varieties of religions techno–lights dynamics.
Dim lights shines the Jewish Faith Menorah.

Copyright © 2007 Geneva M. Neale (Audain)

Funeral Home

Just honoured Mary Jesus' Mom.
Peaceful Funeral Home atmosphere.
Take time to honour all Mothers.
In spite of all short falls.

Those who have had the courage.
Bounce back on and on.
Many moments carried pains.
Distress and chaos lived.
Yes, I stood in front A Coffin.

As I tried to come to term.
This Irish woman's courage.
Tears flowered her face.
She slowly took her fingers.
And crossed her grieving lips.

Copyright © 2007 Geneva M. Neale (Audain)

MAGNETIC FIELD

Life a field of ripened surprises.
Warm water swirls around panels.
Solar panels on top house roofs.
Package reduced at a home show.

Both solar panels now installed.
Kitchen transforms to sunny indoors.
Morning, noon and night brilliance.
Investment cost shines through.

Imagine outdoors turned inside out.
Excited no longer dine in darkness.
God"s natural elements flavoured.
Solar panels modern era venture.

REALIZATIONS

Life Styles our Freedom Movements DREAMS.
Co-relate in mind, body and spirit to be.
Portrayed in faces on every contentent.
Worldwideweb of peoples dying with visions.
Muli-races in stride embraced arm in arm.
Children fearless heads high no smiles.
The message "We shall overcome" we sang.
Universality beams 2006 in our 21st century.
Etched chrystal Lights circulates as stars.
Africans migratation South Africa's diamond.
Segration is Apartied Let Freedom Reign!
Africansin every land struggled nation wide.
Dr. King died for global freedoms' strifes.
Lazar lights showers in every hamlet now.
Our world is interfaced one peoples' pride.
DR. Martin Luther King's REALIZATIONS 2006.

Copyright © 2007 Geneva M. Neale (Audain)

Synchronicity

There is beauty in synchroncity.
Closeness of their equal space.
Between sun and moon and stars
Symmetric cylindrical space

This is termed oneness alignments.
Power and Glory manifest.
A shineless, fearful displaced white moon.
Bungled my neighbour's mind and mine.

Sun and moon both gloriously attracted.
No twinkles from stars in sight.
The sun competed with heated dominance.
The moon now dormant, looked scared.

They correlate in broad daylight.
Metaphysics claims it mystically shines.
Christ's birth at night no coincidence.
Sun, moon and stars synchronously unite.

WORD

In the Beginning the gospel marked word.
Science highest revelation, humans births.
Genesis languages globally revealed.
Breath let us gloriously affirm.
Life rejuvenates spirituality.

Circulate peaceful thoughts in cells.
Imagine life forms with broken minds.
Glorious endearments unite souls.
Youthful delightful feelings spring.
Metaphysical Omnipresence consciousness.

Concealed omniscience depths unfold.
Quiet,omnipotence manages insights.
Flood light faith brilliance from afar.
Remotes illuminate states of souls.

Positive thinkers actively change.
Engage omnipresence look up the word.
Unshakable daffodils in spring romances.
Smile, hugs—renewed hearts, the word love.

Copyright © 2007 Geneva M. Neale (Audain)

ROMANCE

Geneva's poems began as Human Interest: "CUPID", "SMILES," "MY SON", "ONE PENNY", "WHAT", "FREQUENT".

Geneva builds a story that entices, excites with qualities that enhance our lifestyle philosophies.

ADOLESCENCE

Young adults, sons-in-law

Young adults excel balance networks.
Young adults powered individuals.
Multi-races sons-in-law family trees.
Sons or daughters family dynasty.

Active structural decisions beams.
Successful behaviors cultivate.
Journal creative assessments goals.
Activate minuscule cells goals.

Relax great leader Nelson Mandela.
Seniority flaunt ownership maturity.
Evacuate international confidential.
Debate flamboyant armies adolescence.

Copyright © 2007 Geneva M. Neale (Audain)

CUPID IN ORBIT

The Warmth of Cupid's Wings.

Cupid Firefly WINGS embraced our messages.
Temporize keys unlock anxious hearts.
Internal warmth excels feverish temperatures.
Red candied emotions wade around fired minds.

Sensory temperatures heat up our heads.
Feverish warmth changes our blushed skins.
St. Valentine's enormous wishes append.
Cupid zapped feelings of exuberance.

Body shivers, teeth clatter at sixty-five.
Their confidence behold true love springs
Watered eyes sparklingly check valentine cards.
Cupid spirals will orbit again next year.

DIVINE SMILES

Smiles exercise my face; you see!
Relaxed, poised satisfaction to me.
The smiles that lasts forever, we need
Pleasant, pride persuasions on e-mail
Ya man the divine smiles is all to me.

That's when I know the divine smiles
Within me, around me, on net, on line.
My thoughts expand; the work of smiles
Deep within a quiet e-mail tree I see
Ah ha! the divine smiles within me.

Alas! my smiles in www.poetry.com anthology
You think! its geneva? on line you see?
Oh, no not the .com money tree poetry
She is always g e n e n . . . . to me.
Never miss her "divine smiles" personality.

FATHERS' INDETERMINISM

My pa pa passed his golden age 84 in 1997.
What would I want to say to him in 2006?
Our conversations when he remarried at 63.
Three years after Tanty went unto glory, Why?

My mom just died? "I do not need your blessings.
I am your father, you are my child. "Go on!"
"You need to understand, It's not thy will be done."
"But mine to remarry whenever I decide. Goodbye."
My mom just died? "I do not need your blessings.
I am your father, you are my child. "Go on!"
"You need to understand, It's not thy will be done."
"But mine to remarry whenever I decide. Goodbye."

What is all this fuss about Father's day my children asked?
Four successful young adults, fatherless since 1975.
"God forgive all yucky discordant dads' indeterminism
attitudes."

Copyright © 2007 Geneva M. Neale (Audain)

FINAL

Her husband, eighty one, passed.
Their children will eulogize.
His glorious heavenly journey.
Parkinsons traumatized hands.

Her mind is still intact.

She said last rites prayers.

God's will to pray.

Crystal Praying beads embraced.

"Hail Mary and The Lord's Prayer."

Never under-estimate Parkinson's.

Alzheimer's head and heart alive.

Body, mind, spirit mastering tasks.

With styles, thank parents.

Miracles medical break throughs.

Baby boomers fears chaos negotiate.

Generation Xers inherit positive.

Learn the gift of prayers.

In spite of technology skills.

FREQUENT

So you said I can win a winfall eh
That is your key to me
There is the bull
And Here is the Bear
But there is no money for me.

Where is the stocks.com
Where are my shares.html
Well you have my e-mail address
But there is no money for me yet.

FRIENDSHIP

Afro Caribbeans Canadians friendships 1965.
How are you doing these days my friends.
Coconut trees, in an e-mails, are emotional.
Tropical Islands reminders with longings.
Emulate swirling coconut trees branches.
Breathe, exercise, breathe memories sailing.

Steelpans parties limbo on Maracas beach oui.
Hope flows along enthusiastic Trinbago's veins.
Talents cultivate wind blown trees of Life.
Smiles sustain our accomplishments overseas.
Fresh green coconut water we still crave.
Soca rhythms Trinidad and Tobago's invention.

Copyright © 2007 Geneva M. Neale (Audain)

GIFTS

Well, God does answer prayers.
You are blessed on this Good Friday.
Just when I thought.
All had been done by me.
God sends me friendly e-mails.
Via you my friend.
I bless every one.
Whose gifts of strengths I share.
Sometimes, we give luck.
To an unexpected one.
God sent that one, you.
My voice of thanks to you. "Ha!"
So every one guess.
You all are special to me.
Click attachment you will see.

My Son

Love is not a verb you understand?
Weigh all emotions be your soul's guide.
Dignity with step by step vision you become.
Wisdom to know and understand balance.
Build to understand solid foundations.
Deposit cash accounts with no liabilities.
Grow assets to enhance your investments.
Harmonize see yourself financially secure.
Keep away from owing debts to pirates.
Body and mind energies is foremost.
Avoid bowering your cash flows.
Young man invest in markets ownerships.

NOTHINGNESS ASSESSMENT

Our imaginations circulating out in space.
Minds dis-eased organs needs osteopathy.
Dementia seems to transfix humans brains.

Mental deterioration no congratulations.
Millions of families' relationships aflutter.
Humans minds with motor skills disfunctions.

Body, mind and spirit sealed in orbit.
Spirituality land of dreams discovery.
Minds racing around no 'Tower of Babel'.

Affirmations prayers we are in silent unity.
This sacred space, our minds, God's grace.
Global contributions! Thank you alumnae.

POET

I felt quite beautiful as I walked and meditated.
I felt valleys and mountains of this sacred lyricist.
A slope lies flat on earthy floor like a cunning bard.
Earth fashioned like stilts roomy elusive powers felt.

Hillsides earthquakes roar like billowing sheep.
Sensational moles shining within soft drew drops.
Glorious herald illustrate cool slushy pastel rain.
Think Geneva healings streams softly mutter.

Relax final walk amazingly versed in silence.
Marvelous all—inclusiveness restful noiseless walk.
I enjoyed amazements as I stepped off the Labyrinth.
Even as it lies flat on the floor my mind is adrift.

TABLE TOPICS

Picture this table topic blanc lines.
Tropical forests ENCASED IN FIRES.
Outline for new reforesting laws.
Hot visions on blank paper pores.
Rest, observe, clauses resolve.

Sit back regard sweltering effects.
Words evolve into exemplify speeches.
Ream blank pieces of paper ream.
Contentious tropical forests new laws.
Table topics tabled and retable white outs.

Structure table of contents settings.

Self Esteem

My poems on Self-Esteem speak for themselves they tell of barriers; put downs, feeling sad for everyone who cannot obtain the freedoms. We must learn to survive changes in live styles because of skills that must be learned.

In developed countries we are continuously relearning how to handle lots of coping skills with children, relationships as well as interpersonal tolerance in industrial age work places. Self Esteem teaches us that we must all deal with challenges.

Mantra "This or something better when life seems dark and we must decide to make changes in our charts new directions where we must turn back or go around issues or go beyond the end of any challenging issues in our lifestyles."

Great modern thought forms use meditations that are found in every religion on the face of this earth. Life style forces allow us to have the will to look back at what can be felt within our body, head and feelings. We change our thoughts to begin again and again it teaches us to know to set new goals periodically or frequently.

We are learning coping skills from previous era as if we are in the cave peopling days off Egypt or off Africa or far Eastern places where civilization began. The Old testaments changes from the dark ages. Even in tales of the Medieval times there were coping skills about captured dynasties evolvements in those books.

We learn from eastern philosophers what allows our self-esteem benefits. My searches to find my self-esteem I read "The Power of Positive Thinking." I learn from short motivational emotional types of digital tapes. Relax mind, soul and body. So that those deep rock thoughts caused me to get transform.

I am in management of emotions. I have grown my knowledge to change selfish circumstances to successful achievements. Copyright Geneva M. Neale (Audain) rewrite 2012

Poetry by Geneva M. Neale (Audain), Copyright Geneva M. Neale (Audain)

ALIGHT ILLUMINATING SELF WORTH

Mothers heard "we'll amount to nothing."
Older women cannot do a thing.
Mother accept your obligations.
Empty millions of insults gathered.

Mothers grow new thoughts daily.
Mothers remembers each pregnancy.
Millions of unpleasant feelings.
Fraught with supreme discomforts.

Was it nine or seven months?
Girls transformed to women.
Girls developed mothers' personalities.
'ALight illuminating talents.

Women's latent scheduled unveilings.
Release negative, untangle partners.
Discard opinions locked in storage.
Today we stand on various platforms.

Unveil 'Alight Illuminating Selfworth.'
Mothers ditch, feeble intrusive treadmills.
Unharnes pentup ideas, abusers put downs.
Motivate 'Alight illuminating Selfworth.'

Copyright © 2007 Geneva M. Neale (Audain)

Cultures of Invisible Women

Status of Women 2001 WINNERS
Selection, excitements,freedoms UNTOLD
Women of Status goal setters NOW KNOWN

Women challenged VOICES UNHEARD UNSEEN
Women achievers MEDIATERS, HUMAN BEIGNS
Women who aim ON BOARD SPACE SHIPS IN SPACE

Women of Status not CHATTELS, YES,INVESTORS
Prosthesis computer chips INSTALLERS
Women temporary/ONGOING ACHIEVERS

Women of Status CONGRATULATIONS ALL WON
WOMEN KNOWLEDGE IN EQUITY AND EQUALITY
Women of Status OUR CENTENNIAL GLORIES

Women of Status nominees, YOU REJOICE
Women KEY NOTE SPEAKERS, ADVOCATERS.
Women of Status DIAMOND ACHIEVERS.

25th Anniversary SMOOZE, RENUNION, APPLAUSE
NEW CITY OF Hamilton, Ontario. WOMEN RISE!
Mayor's Status of Women Committee AWARD 2001

Copyright © 2007 GENEVA M. NEALE

DIAMOND RACE RELATIONS

Race relations Month.
Encased Diamonds rails under ground.
God's intricate stones creations.

Million dollars diamond gems industry.
Harvested treasures—women best friend.
Rythmical tribes songs migrants return home.

Labour implemented race relations in minds.
Africa dense multi-coloured universe awaits.
South Africa's multi million diamond mines.

Dysfunctional minds like thunder explode.
Mandatory XRay cameras technology films.

Employees souls emptied sole to sole.
Diamonds encased unpolished stones.
Gen's Life emerges, Gen the African's gem.

ONE PENNY

A SEED FELL ON MY LAWN TODAY
THIS SEED WAS CHANGED INTO A BILL
A MILLION DOLLAR BILL BEGAN WITH JUST ONE
HUNDRED
MILLION PENNIES IT WOULD SEEM
TURN ONE EXTREME PLAY INTO A WINDFALL
ALL THINGS ARE CONNECTED WITH JUST ONE
LITTLE PENNY

Copyright © 2007 GENEVA M. NEALE

Online Inventors

Divine orders for partnerships online.
Women must initiate goals inventories.
Faith ongoing legacy investments provide.
Love is a universal spiral spiritual mobile.

Moods swings surround harbours amber sunrise.
Volunteer opportunities surpass human dares.
Life supports reinvert positives to radiate.
Inject omnipresence in levee embankments.

No obstacles in looks, meditate skywards.
Crybaby never, opportunities bloom for ever.
Seductions options or confrontations choices.
Decision made, never vacillate horah, horah!

Woman inconsequential facade beautified.
Incorporated speeches toast their confidence.
Seniors again review commitments to embark.
Renegotiate family trees growth orchestrate.

Banish relationships encounters up the Nile.
Evade moody behaviours become the prig.
Expand senior moments over new horizons float.
Improve egotistic formulas in each blueprint.

SELF ESCALATION

One never think self escalation until.
The dawn of facial changes are happening.
What is youth about hormones or testosterone?
Life begins with my elevating myself I AM woman.

Lift myself beyond zero like yeast of self escalation.
Sky scrapers elevations lifts my esteem beyond.
Not one misdirected energy zooming in.
Way above me I know I am the bright light.

I AM looking forward at 40, 50, 60 and beyond.
I Am the best person I Am yet to become.
You have not seen my I Am portfolio as yet.
Locked inside my breasts that suckled children.

How can you understand me you never asked me.
Like mahogany trees primed at 50 years and over.
Like a lounge built a hundred and fifty years ago.
Like a love settees extraordinaire characteristics.

Furniture primed from natural oils in trees pores.
Demisting myths womanhood attaining goals in 69th year.
As Charlie tells tales of cream raising to the top yet again.

Copyright © 2009 Geneva M. Neale (Audain)

SELF ESTEEM

Women in global delivery wards.
Gallant gentlemen thuds.
Tears flow Lab tests positive.
Behave in sociable manners.
Women Shreik Nurse OOH.
Muffled gossips full term.
Women's stories silenced.
What you are pregnant again.
I love you but this is insane.
Women decide in captivity.

Conceptions fantasized by men.
Morning sickness is no joke.
Women beautify yourselves.
Women focus on 'New Thoughts.
No longer profanities SHREIK.
Build constructive dynasties.
Motivative, educate, inspire.
Women love each child conceive.
Set goals you will succeed.
Ownership of your selfesteem.

WHAT

EXCLAIMATION! WHAT!
QUESTION? WHAT?
ANSWER smooth what.
Thrilling WHAT, WHAT, WHAT.

Amazed, at the exclaimation what!
Surprised, by the answer what?
Excited, by the evasive voice. what.
Say what? You mean the excited what.

Annoyed What! Get lost what.
Or just a coming on musical what.
Saying the word What? Can mean a lot.
One might even loose quite a lot. WHAT!

Travel to the Caribbean "Whah 'appen mah?"
A greeting by all, "Wah happen dey man."
"Ay Whah or whoh yoh doing deh girl?"
Say what? You don't say! What do you mean?

BIOGRAPHY

Photo © copyright 2007 Graham Gordon

Geneva was born in The Town of San Juan in Trinidad, however her parents settled down in Cascade Village on the outskirts of Port of Spain where she attended Ideal High School. Even at an early age, she excelled in English literature and Poetry.

In her final year of high school, Saturday mornings were a pleasure for her to meet with five students for The Poetry Club as an extracurricular hobby. The students were selected because they had a peaked interest in English Poets.

Geneva recalled that the teacher referred to Poetry as the Romance Language. Hmmmm . . . the girls could not even watch any of the boys in the class tight restrictions. There was not any **First Kiss Poetry Writing** in the school building or outside the building either!

Life's experiences amongst the cascading falls is what makes Geneva's poems sizzle . . . the brilliance of acquired self esteem from various metaphysical principles of ancient and modern philosophers.

- Geneva studied Human Services Management and graduated from McMaster University in 1998, at the age of almost 60!

- The Daily Word published in the 1890's by Charles and Myrtle Fillmore allowed Geneva to understand that bible teachings allow you to makeover your life to create a productive lifestyle.

- As her beliefs system went through social adjustments they fired elements within her head, body, mind and soul.

- She began to rise above the ashes of self-doubts and peer controls,

Thoughts management skills in the principles of "seek and you can find" became her goal to pursue enrichment in her life skills.

AWARDS AND REVIEWS

Geneva Audain was born in San Juan, Trinidad. Attended Ideal High School in Trinidad completed her final Grade 12 equivalent examinations. Geneva Audain participated in youth organization in the Island of Trinidad with the Tranquility Methodist Church Organizations as a Church member, Sunday School teacher, Choir member, Girls League President. Each activity of this International Organization functions were submitted to Methodist Church Head Quarters in England.

Note: Trinidad and Tobago had been a member of the British Common Wealth. Trinidad and Tobago celebrated its independence in 1963,

Geneva Neale then got married in 1964. Geneva M. Neale (Audain) has been recognized for her work both as a community volunteer and as an international poet. She has been given the Outstanding Achievement Award in Poetry by the www.poetry.com International Society of Poets from 2002 through to 2007. 2012 poetry.com is under new management.

Several of Geneva M. Neale (Audain) poetry are published in the International Society of Poetry Anthology in various editions since 2000.

Outstanding Achievement Award 2005

Outstanding Achievement Award 2006

Geneva's presentation DVD of THE PASSION & THE POETRY expressions of her spoken words. Geneva's poetry set within a fantasy of The little people and creatures of the Cascading Forests; as in the great tradition of Hans Christian Anderson and the mystical spirit of life communications to her son, daughters, remembrance of her father and her mother, her thoughts of money talents and a philosophy of the decent good of love, life and tamed common sense personality of Geneva M. Neale (Audain)

Retired, divorced mother four successful goal oriented children as a single parent.

Juno Award band son Haydain Neale achieved his final goal to win 'Three' Canadian Music JUNO Awards to cancer. RIP November 22, 2012. MY SON dedicated to her son 2007.

Links://www.thepassionandthepoetry.com

Order Geneva's DVD Now!

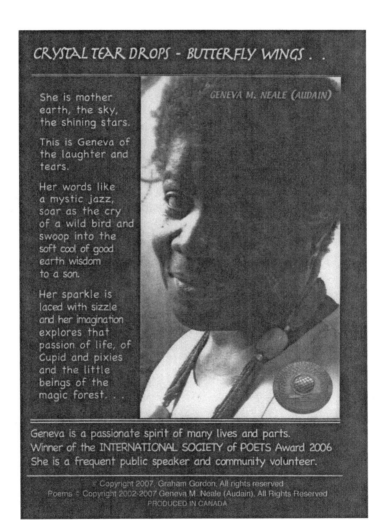

Go to this website http://www.thepassionandthepoetry.com/ to see samples of Geneva's DVD and her most recent works.

Email: **geneva@thepassionandthepoetry.com**

DVD Front Cover

$ **29.99 CAD**
plus $ 4.00 shipping & handling.

Top of Form

Bottom of Form

DVD Back Cover

CRYSTAL TEAR DROPS—BUTTERFLY WINGS . . .

She is the mother earth, the sky, the shining stars.

This is Geneva of the laughter and tears.

Her words like a mystic jazz, soar as the cry of a wild bird and swoop into the soft cool of good earth wisdom to a son.

Her sparkle is laced with sizzle and her imagination explores that passion of life, of Cupid and pixies and the little beings of the magic forest . . .

This remarkable DVD captures the sizzling creative magic of Geneva and provides a memoir of her growing up in Cascading Forests of Trinidad in the days of World War II rations.

In her own words, Geneva describes poetically her very first kiss and the stunning awakening of womanhood in marriage which includes discoveries of single motherhood and the responsibility of becoming that tough, wise spirit of guidance for 4 children.

DVD produced by Award Winner Graham Gordon.

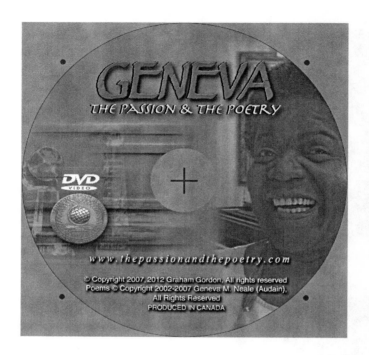

Geneva is a passionate spirit of many lives and parts.
Winner of the INTERNATIONAL SOCIETY of POETS AWARD
2006 and again in 2007, she is a frequent public speaker and
community volunteer.

http://www.thepassionandthepoetry.com/

Email: **geneva@thepassionandthepoetry.com**

CPSIA information can be obtained at www.ICGtesting.com
Printed in the USA
LVOW071520100313

323521LV00004B/547/P